D1218262

TOOLS FOR TEACHERS

- **ATOS:** 0.6
- **GRL:** B
- **WORD COUNT:** 34

- **CURRICULUM CONNECTIONS:**
  animals, habitats

Skills to Teach

- **HIGH-FREQUENCY WORDS:** a, here, on, who
- **CONTENT WORDS:** bear, goat, hawk, moose, mountain, puma, yak
- **PUNCTUATION:** periods, question marks
- **WORD STUDY:** broad /o/, spelled *aw* (*hawk*); *r*-controlled vowels (*bear*); long /o/, spelled *oa* (*goat*); dipthong /ou/ (*mountain*); schwa /ə/, spelled *ai* (*mountain*); long /oo/, spelled oo (*moose*), u (*puma*)
- **TEXT TYPE:** information report

Before Reading Activities

- Read the title and give a simple statement of the main idea.
- Have students "walk" though the book and talk about what they see in the pictures.
- Introduce new vocabulary by having students predict the first letter and locate the word in the text.
- Discuss any unfamiliar concepts that are in the text.

After Reading Activities

Ask the children to think about the environment and the animals mentioned in the book. What other mountain animals can they name? What else do they know about these animals?

Tadpole Books are published by Jump!, 5357 Penn Avenue South, Minneapolis, MN 55419, www.jumplibrary.com

Copyright ©2018 Jump. International copyright reserved in all countries. No part of this book may be reproduced in any form without written permission from the publisher.

Editorial: Hundred Acre Words, LLC **Designer:** Anna Peterson

Photo Credits: Dreamstime: Christopher Lindner, 12–13; Esben Hansen, cover. Shutterstock: asylysun, 6–7; Daniel Prudek, 14–15; Dmitry Pichugin, 2–3; Gary K Gray, 4–5; Igumnova Irina, 8–9; Marc Bruxelle, 1; Richard Seeley, 6–7; Scenic Shutterbug, 10–11.

Library of Congress Cataloging-in-Publication Data
Names: Fretland VanVoorst, Jenny, 1972– author.
Title: Who lives on a mountain? / by Jenny Fretland VanVoorst.
Description: Minneapolis, Minnesota: Jump!, Inc., 2017. | Series: Who lives here? | Includes index. | Audience: Age 3 to 6.
Identifiers: LCCN 2017032117 (print) | LCCN 2017035160 (ebook) | ISBN 9781624967283 (ebook) | ISBN 9781620319598 (hardcover: alk. paper) | ISBN 9781620319604 (pbk.)
Subjects: LCSH: Mountain animals—Juvenile literature.
Classification: LCC QL113 (ebook) | LCC QL113 .F74 2017 (print) | DDC 591—dc23
LC record available at https://lccn.loc.gov/2017032117

WHO LIVES ON A MOUNTAIN?

by Jenny Fretland VanVoorst

TABLE OF CONTENTS

Who Lives on a Mountain?. 2

Words to Know. 16

Index. 16

tadpole
books

WHO LIVES ON A MOUNTAIN?

Who lives on a mountain?

A goat lives here.

hawk

A hawk lives here.

bear

A bear lives here.

A puma lives here.

moose

A moose lives here.

A yak lives here.

WORDS TO KNOW

bear

goat

hawk

moose

puma

yak

INDEX

bear 9

goat 5

hawk 7

moose 13

mountain 3

puma 11

yak 15